Mailing Letters
To the
Moon

By
Neva Flores

For My Beautiful Daughter
Amber Nicole Bowden

Table of Contents

Table of Contents
(Continued)

Table of Contents
(Continued)

Table of Contents
(Continued)

Mailing Letters to the Moon

Before you can feel the soft touch of poetry
and it can play a song for you,
look for the positive aspect in moonlit shadows.
Stop and wonder how a heart breaks then makes friends
who give of themselves
until they bleed out on the cold floors
of the world.

Do you find that time lays heavy on you
within dreams where snow melts in pictures
of piercing eyes, that mail letters to the moon?
Or, are you afraid to look out the window
and stop pretending
you are falling in love with being all alone
with just your heart and a slingshot?

What litters the path where your feet move?
Calls out to the sky
that there is no magic wish staring at you
waiting for you to finish.
Does your breath catch in conversations
held with snowflakes
that spin and bow then fade away?
Leaving you to wonder where you go from here.

Has it come to the point where you walk in places
where white lies run through the stream of life?
Does your innocence struggle with colors?
Making your eyes believe nothing is true
when something new becomes old
inside of winds creeping and
freezing like icicles.

Before you can feel the soft touch of poetry
and it can play a song for you,
you must have walked this path
I have described.
Do not stand up and leave with your
thoughts racing, climbing higher and higher,
lest you become one of those hearts
that bleed.

Building Bridges Over the Silence of Disbelief

In hopes, someone would sing my thoughts
while breathing in
a tantalizing dance,
I painted an existence with hands full
of shining light.
I waited for my heart's desire
to come to life
running in my blood and spirit
like an army's last advance.

The Earth is something that holds my emotions
upon rippling waves
of healing winds,
streaming to me in an isolated dance.
Yet, sometimes
I get lost in the night sky
and find myself cursing the pain
while sitting on the grounds of today's truth
and circumstance.

My hands seek reasons to forgive
the silence of disbelief,
while catching secrets that have been
thrown away.
Even if I nailed the windowsill
of confusion shut,
my heart would still care about tomorrow
However, my mind
could not be changed
nor swayed.

Waiting For My Heart to Break in Two

Oh, to feel my breath inside of what
has not been touched in years
by the breezes I find, as if meant to be my air.

After the sunset fades, I cannot express
how it feels to have your heart break in two.
To hear a song for days that still loves you in the morning.

Flying straight through the tinted glass
I hold on tight to the place I know
is standing in the distance.
In search of one, whose notions move into shadows
loyal only to an army of water
that is sitting back and looking at every word
as if it is an ocean
of a single heartbeat.

I sing this song in my heart
with my eyes closed,
never bitter, but you know that.
I hold no shame of the memories
held dear. Their touch whispers
like a smear of warm sun
promising not to forget
what it searches for.

Smiling into eternity's cup,
I begin to write.
I write of dancing in the windows
where the sun and moon
are uninhibited as they drink from the air
of unmeasured words.

A place where the only thing I wish for
is a glimpse of flowers
that will push the thoughts of waiting
for my heart to break in two
.…away.

Acceptance Is a Difficult Thought

In all of the directions
of what you want to tell me
comes anything
looking better in motion.
Although I am torn by the reasons
I try hard to project
fact is,
there are moments
I yield to emotion.

I can relax out of earshot
of any kind of danger.
That does not scatter
or burn anyone else.
Yet, I am not meaning to remember
Why all the hours acknowledge what I do not know,
because I won't tell myself.

Acceptance, my sweetheart
is a difficult thought.
Believe me, I know what has to be done.
While one is being held
under the watchful eye of the hand
tightly holding Love's gun.

Some Eyes Seek Beautiful Shadows

I know that some eyes seek beautiful shadows to follow
What suffering highlighted by moonlight can do
How the stain of the world fills spaces in our hearts
Until we no longer notice, we cannot feel the fire
Of what is right and true

I know how whispers of our past can take our earthly peace
Until we become tossed like disheveled leaves
How it feels to speak and think no one is listening
The terrifying feat of trying to be strong
When I want to grieve

I know those dark nights of looking down empty hallways
When I am afraid to breathe or close my eyes
As if a spell has been cast on my life in subtle shades
With a power that I cannot wish away
No matter how I sigh

However, I also know how we wait to make a single move
Day to day how we sit still and just abide
Pushing away all hands of comfort while asking
Why all the stars have been removed
From our skies

Making Bricks

So many things cry out to my heart
as I look into the sky.
I see ten thousand tears falling unsatisfied
from a heaven,
that has left the pain of every day
still felt when breathing in
a new dawn's
wondrous rays of light.

Shadows clearly lay awake
murmuring undiscovered truths.
Sending looks and smiles
with all of their demands.
While they watch, the curtains close on many lives
who never took a chance to look outside
of what they did not understand.

Bricks are placed one by one
around the love we hold inside.
Until forever, becomes a word that drifts away.
Into all the tears falling unsatisfied among shadows.
Lying awake crying out to my heart,
"No more straw and clay."

Burning Letters I Never Wrote

Keeping please and thank you
within the answers held far
from talking eyes.
Is a burst of air splashing casually
from the pages of a book,
waltzing into sighs.

I just saw indignation
standing out in a thin smile again.
Emotionless laughter is at my door
with another sign, still and pausing
when night has entered
silently my friend.

On one side little boxes full of hope
grow bigger as they sit.
Yet, misting gently in the distance
comes the morning instinctively
they grow smaller then quit.

I do not know where I should be walking
or if I should mention what I see.
When uncertainty brings a little chill
hardens this soft heart I carry inside of me.

You may hear stones from the ground
drinking the truth from my hands.
However, not if you still have
an axe to grind, Stupidities Pipe to smoke
at your command.

Listen to the cries of no, no, no
breathing inside all human souls.
Close your eyes and pretend
you are in Disneyland burning letters, I sent you
but never wrote.

Your breath will come in a whispered kiss,
running through your head. The poison
from your mouth will empty out into all goodbyes
you meant, but never said.

Words Have Eyes that Sing

Do you turn away from eyes that sing
on nights filled with emotion?
Never wondering if you could drown
in your imagination.
Without understanding all the poetry
dancing in your heart
warming words of choice,
in your tongue of fascination.

Do your hours exist in a sky familiar
with moments such as these?
Is there nowhere to look
for heaven free of possession?
Where words do not cry out
to be contemplated
by your pen
to become lovely music
giving light to your obsession.

Can one learn to be absent
from this transparent house of glass?
Remove the flowing ink
running through their veins?
Still breathe, without giving out
a subtle handful of their soul
each time a word calls out
to be painted in a refrain?

I cannot turn from eyes that sing
on nights filled with emotion.
My heaven is this possession
in which I freely drown.
You may not understand the poetry
dancing in my heart
still I will write,
until again I am dust……
in the ground.

My Lips Fall upon Your Thoughts

If my lips appear to fall upon your thoughts,
that is where
they are supposed to be.
At night,
When your ears hear pages
of the faintest verse
whispering on your neck,
it is my way of telling you everything
will be all right,
go back to sleep,
it is just me.

If you feel the softest kiss in the morning
as if the sun has filled the passageways
of your heart with everything, you miss.
The radiance you feel in these spaces
is not a dream in which you have fallen,
nor random chance,
it is my way
of sending, you bliss.

If your temperature rises in a delightful instant,
eternally warming your soul
with a drink
and leaving your heart glowing.
It is because it holds the promises
my heart placed long ago
in a chalice called my love
where you can drink
of a warmth overflowing.

I am always with you
even on those nights
that seems to never end.
I walk delicately across your mind
tying the strings of your heart
to my own.

You can hear my voice
when my lips fall upon your thoughts
whispering, "I love you, My Heart,
I'm coming home."

Count the Stars in Silence

Cover the touch wandering in and out
of the brightest tides of time
because the splendor of diamonds
will run away
leaving you with empty hands that sigh.
Let your voice light everything
that shakes your blessings,
so that you may live,
continue standing
never hide.

Count the stars in silence,
get lost
in their features
as you dream of holding hands
with the tides of time.
You will find yourself in flight
over roads that meet years
full of deep eyes
with no tears.
Countless thoughts you will treasure,
raining down
in perfect rhyme.

Bid farewell to your trust in wealth
it can die before your eyes.
Cover the touch
of the brightest tides of time.
Count the stars in silence
when you fly over the roads
of your memories.
A strong breeze
will blow into your thoughts,
sweet
as the finest wine.

When Everything is Fine is Only Said in Shame

The passing strokes of my heart remain
on the canvas of the world.
Waves of love watch
as it paints an ambitious mirage,
faintly touching the realms of comfort.

Where does the beginning of dreams blow
to the west or the north?
Today's pain seeps upon the seconds
and I breathe a sigh
into the winds of happiness and warmth.

The small things, once again, float
into unlit frames
that looks into your eyes
and then the worlds.
While our spirits refrain from wishing lies
were not deliberately told.

Light swears it is hungry
and doesn't know
it is flickering like a faithful poem,
pushing to speak out
about itself.
Traveling along with truth
that has been tossing stones.

Lyrics say I love you
and then cry to the back of guilt
because it stared at you in a sense of wonder
when they were wrote.
In an atmosphere
without meter or rhyme.

The taste of a glimpse of wings
leaves painted lips
dancing in the flames.
Unbound memories are more than we know
when everything is fine
is only said in shame.

Where Are Your Words?

Where have you been with your words
you vowed to whisper softly?
Until they tumbled over the moon.
Tranquil images are all I can see
in your rhymes
that sank deep into the night
too soon.

Where are the eyes that lit up my world?
and filled my pockets
with dreams of a life that shines?
I am realizing now
What I once was
you have steadily changed
as you exhaled your lines.

Is my hope a golden thought
I love because it dwells
in my emotions
becoming a journey
where I drop to my knees,
spelling out words
then wonder where they lead
into my own circumstances?

Sometimes, when I sleep,
I glide over shells,
holding the hand of life,
forming collages, I could never forget
even when I am weary and I speak
of past things I should have forgotten
over the years.

Where have you been with your words
that makes me smile in knowing
I have found my safe harbor
where I can be quiet
and revel in the tranquil images
you create
in my heart and soul.

The Earth is Still Warm

When I am not with you,
the earth is still warm
from hours that are seen no more.
I can feel the rhythm of yesterday
asking questions
when everything collects on the currents
of our own shadows.

I cast last night among the hills
where we were young and thoughtless
peered above the words
standing
before my eyes.
Where butterflies lived inside a song
waiting
for the world to sing.

Looking to tell a story
somehow different
from any ever written down,
I began unlocking the mysteries of life.
I found that the beauty
of growing old
had kept its secrets well,
from my ears.

In the middle of the wonder
there must surely
lay a seed of hope in the meadows
where you and I saw fireflies
in the still of night.
Perhaps there,
we can still hear the echo
of its footsteps.

Eternity wanders through my mind
seeking praise
while the breath of truth
shows the world its strong arms.
Life awakens
to close the door on lessons learned
and yet, the earth
is still warm.

Melody of a Perfect Smile

Flowers are hung over the voices
where hope is not denied.
A story of unimaginable innocence
has been embraced
and now sings a melody
of a perfect smile
that has become one
with the skies.

Life laughs and takes flight
while violins play
for the stars,
chasing storms of fear
until our mouths speak its words
no more.
We wait with doves
we feed by hand
as we rejoice
on golden shores.

The depth of forever
knows
that no sadness
shall make waves or leave symbols
in our minds
that cannot fly away.
Together we will celebrate innocence
rippling
through our days.

Sinking Into the Night

I am willing to sink into the sound
of night's changing secrets.
Where the world sees my breath
wipe away the tears mirroring its pain.
Smiles are caught on fire,
wooed by this poet,
nevertheless, they do not
reflect the same.

Instead of playing under trees,
I allow everything to be swept away
by the winds,
on the soft petals of a voice.
A voice that empties all its brilliance
into our sleep,
comes to see our smiles rejoice.

Life is exhibited in dirt
from the bottom of my shoe
yet never utters a word.
Still, I will never wave goodbye
to thoughts that turn.
Does anyone ever really understand
the smiles a poet burns?

I welcome hands that hush the existence
of whispered memories.
Lighting candles dwelling in our minds.
If you knew what was on the line,
would you be willing to sink
into night's sound
in kind?

Reality of Your Fantasy

You delight in the presence of a moment in heaven
where you are invincible
within your colorful memories.
It is here you dance to sounds moving in reply
from hills, you drove to the sea.

Do you realize that your laughter can melt hearts?
However, that it isn't a crime to not sit alone
in your pain? Your mystique points a finger
at your smile and the frown in your eyes
the same.

Many hearts have spaces
where the world has lit candles
as a sacrificial move of their own heartbeat.
Yet, our own desire to hold on tight
to skeletons of discontent
readily admits defeat.

In days long past
you filled two cups with ease.
Yet, when given the choice
of filling three,
you set a trail ablaze
Remembering the hidden reasons
why your hands should be set free.

Yes, you delight in the presence
of a moment in heaven
where you are invincible
within your colorful memories.
I only hope you will not be forever snared
in the reality of your fantasy.

You have chilled the spaces in your heart
by blocking out the rays of life
when you sit alone in your rain.
None can claim to know
your heart
yet, many are willing
to share your pain.

Ink in the Wind

I tremble when I hear the voice of the wind saying,
"Why should I even care
if my actions close the eyes
of those who yield to me?"
and all that I know
is that here I stand with pen in hand
in a world of my own making,
contemplating
a potential stalemate.

The time has come and whispers to me
from the lips of the universe
that the stairs of the fiercest storm
are covered with everything
that I have hidden in my mind.
Confusion attempts to run
through my veins creating a madness
with fingers
oh so unkind.

I gaze at the warm sun and wonder how
I lost the desire
I had in my younger days
to bravely sing to the world
from a throat that has not forgotten
how it feels to stand in the gap.
Nor what it takes to expose wind
that does not care
whom its actions destroy.

With pen in hand I speak to the wind
with words the same as if
I called upon
twelve thousand angels
whose wings float upon each gale
as if they were merely
a part of a beautiful dream.
Once again, I feel safe
in this world of my own making.
My trembling ends.

Dreams of Unknown Melodies

Dreams of unknown melodies become my companions
when the moon sits upon her throne, my love.
Far away, more gravitating
are the quivering stars in the heavens
up above.

My life floats within the sun in a blissful perfect peace.
Blazing there, high above the tallest trees.
In lines, my soul can name
running ceaseless and as fair as fair
can be.

Within all the perfect strength I find from these two,
there lies this land, where breezes blow.
To chase away the fog
softly creeping across my heart,
with woe.

The cares of life are swept away in unknown melodies
into that place known as wilderness, of sound.
My eyes are turned to touch
upon their ancient realms of hope.
Once again……….
my world is spinning round.

Within Forms of Silent Time

In the blossoming winds of life
we are scattered,
within forms of silent time.
On all those nights where love
Is more than flesh
holding our will.
The foundation we build
is yours and mine.

Defeat is a precarious lantern
who's light
is bitterly bright and unfair.
Yet nothing
can spring from rivers
I call mine,
that could ever make me
forsake you and go there.

Discontent will never be mine
to hold.
Because I know you understand
all these words
I carve
from my heart.
My spirit
is at your command.

You are the morning
that quenches my thirst.
My fragrance
after the rain.
How could I ever forget you
or these sighs you left
here in my heart
to remain?

Hand of Sorrow

When you found pleasure
walking on the bridge of night
you did not breathe in
the eyes that cried.
You gave your heart
to the dreams of midnight,
all for the want of sighs.

You lived beside
the cause of never. In a garden
beautiful as the reasons why.
I never mentioned the winds
of all your years,
always trusting, one day
you would fly.

You searched for sleep
by haunting ways
no tear first had been.
Time passed, left you singing
an endless song
of dreams of midnight
on that bridge again.

Your world had no time
where rain fell
in crystal showers.
In vain you burned
to become a part
of skies that whispered
words of honey
into your every hour.

When you found pleasure
walking on the bridge of night.
You found the hand of sorrow.
You gave your heart
to the dreams of midnight.
The eyes that cried,
found your tomorrow.

Starting a Fire with Ink from My Pen

It started with a fire
built with young leaves
and the ink from my pen.
Whether it is your fault or my own,
our lives are intertwined
in the flame.
Still, the breath of our moon
carries a message
to us both;
never offer up the slightest wave
of shame.

Calling from the ground is the rain
that found the wind
that blew paper from my hands.
A wind that practiced
a religion of picking up pieces
of broken hearts
and throwing them back down,
only to kiss their cries
with a stampede
of what they cannot understand.

A well thought out plan started out
with a fire built
with young leaves
and the ink from my pen.
It is not your fault,
nor is it mine.
If we can we ever stop listening
to the winds
that kiss the cries of our broken hearts,
from the flame, we could come
un-entwined.

Uncut

A soft image satisfies the deepest sea
found in your eyes,
is recognized as comfort.
Harmony makes a new wind flow lovingly
into the arms
of old wounds suffered.

Measured out. our shores bend
to meet in passion
to taste time's recurrent goals.
Lighted, I talk with my hands
to find balance
shimmering within my soul.

Scenes pass by of places
with nowhere to go,
sailing as tributes
tired of singing chords
without gain.
Still, I smile magically
as if I am bound to live life
uncut, yet emptied of all pain.

Presence of Warmth

I touched the presence of warmth on my pillow
it made me feel sure that I was safe,
went back to sleep smoother than my heartbeat.
I awoke to find myself hidden
behind memories of you.

Standing on the corner of never say no,
my feet are firmly planted
in I cannot say I am sorry.
Now I wonder, if I will I be the rock
laying here asking myself
where I found this bitter pill
under my tongue.

Did I sleep while it rained
on everything, we ever had?
Until nothing but sand existed
inside all of these silent moments.
When bluebirds sang
about how the stars laugh
was I here drowning
in my own pride?

I touched the presence of warmth on my pillow,
then I reached out to yours
felt the cold.
I lay here listening to the rain
falling smoother than my heartbeat,
I have never felt,
so alone.

Shattering the Mirror to Nowhere

The wind moves over understanding,
enjoying its time away
from tears,
feels complete again.
Sleep, I am sure, sets sail
with a stranger,
breaking the shell
enveloping your pillow,
taking away pain.

Colors give you a taste of brightness
eternity goes through
when blushing
at its own progress.
While forever struggles
with patience
touching upon fruit,
once thought of as undressed.

Cold water comes near,
turns round and round
graciousness.
Extending waves
of grace's touch.
Walking the halls
pressed against a smile
that say's "I am sorry",
no one notices
quite so much.

Long, long after our experiences
caress the light
we have given time,
they are unfolded,
carried away.
Insistence shatters
the mirror to nowhere,
sending winds of understanding,
my way.

Spun Web of Gypsy Invitation

New colors embrace the memory of life's soil
while looking at promises
rushing through our veins.
A tune is heard from our hearts'
circling places in time
where our eyes become the surface
of our souls,
greeting what we see floating
on the winds
of change.

If we are clearly visible as separate bodies
held on a spun web of gypsy invitation,
why then do we only remember
the perfect peace
of how our minds meet?
You touch each breath I draw in,
as if hunting down my despair
until it becomes as smoke
with leaving feet.

Before the stars were chiseled into an age
that held us captive,
sleep was where the light of the moon
played innocently.
Father Fate swirls, renames himself
with each breath I take,
keeping time for the promises
of true love
that still sing out
to you and me.

I Will Be There to See

I will be in the valley
where the sand meets the tree of fire
and walls that close in
do not exist.
My arms have become part of the stars.
When I walk they enfold night
with a web encircling a kiss.

My heart contains a spirit of love
I obtained from the sea,
when my skies were filled
with all that I know.
I am here in the valley in between time
and the place where the tree of fire
still glows.

Come and take my hand
when your morning is cold,
until all that is left
is how you remember me.
Then, when you look into the glass
where your face was alone,
I will always be there
to see.

High Above Our Never

Lightning strikes and shifts high above our never.
Time flows like a river standing out in delight.
There is more power within ideas
pressing against the throat of morning;
filling your life's cup with wonder,
than when dusk stands alone
dressed only
in feathered flight.

You cannot pry open the fingers of flight
make them advance any higher
even if you want to know
about time that's passed.
Twisting and turning you will begin falling,
until what you want to be
sweeps across this land.
Take my hand
perhaps we will learn
the truth at last.

Last night you looked better
than the first time I met you.
All the while familiar feelings
sank into our sleep.
Madness streams into a waterfall of self,
full of imperfection.
Where comfort causes passion
to stretch tenderly
into each word you kiss,
when our talk
runs ever deep.

All the tears that fall between rocks
surrounding your loneliness
want you to try hard
feel nothing at all.
They glisten as they attempt to become
lost inside your stubborn heart.
Forever tells me these tears
will continue as trails on faces,
and be heard as thunder
when they fall.

One

I am who you see
when you look in the mirror.
What you hold
inside your heart.
I am the same as you are,
I am your other part

Our hearts are one
and the same,
I look inside and see you.
You look back
and see yourself
in everything I do.

We are two hearts
that beat as one
separately together.
My heart has found a home
in yours
where it will stay forever.

A Deep Breath

She said to lie still
let my thoughts take a deep breath,
until memories
were all that remained.
However, she did not know
I carry treasures
that drift in and out of my mind
like the tide of the ocean.
Which can never be contained.

She told me that I could block out
the words that I write.
The ones I now know by heart that wait.
She said they were only a habit
I had formed in time.
She did not know the words
would only keep flowing
she had spoken too little, too late.

I told her of your embrace
of the first moment with you.
How your eyes never drift from my own.
Then I watched as she saw
your heart in my eyes
writing the words
that can never stop flowing
within me.
She took a deep breath,
and soon
she was gone.

A Loner's Heart Dances In the Ink

The sky's nose is pressed
to the window
of a loner's heart.
Knowing something dances
in the bottom
standing in front of him.

Nothing in life shows
what a loner really feels,
more than
that fountain of ink
whispering from her pen.

Still the sky wonders
if there is anything
really there.
Or, if a loner's heart
is merely full of emptiness
dancing bare.

You can see the sky's ear
pressed ever so closely,
against the window
of a loner's heart.
Listening to the pulsing beat
that flows.

The sky knows something wondrous
dances in the bottom.
That it is timeless,
yet still he wonders if
it will still dance
in the ink if he finds it.

Unearth

Expectations agony
deep inside my mind.
Has reached a point
of no return.
What is this you do to me?
All of this that burns.

Neither logic, lies,
nor sense does it make.
I care not
for what I see is true.
True it feels and must be
the answer lies in you.

Alleviation of curiosity
is a must.
To calm what rages
deep inside.
No peace left as is.
Unearth
or come untied.

A Dot

What if I am wrong about tomorrow
and the day before?
Everything I think is true,
I find is not.
Will my world just stop revolving,
spinning all around
If I discover,
that I am just a dot?

A dot among the billions,
existing in this day,
thinking that we all hold the truth.
That everything we know inside
is self-evident
and we don't give a damn
about the proof

What if I find that my beliefs
are just a fairy tale,
a mystical illusion
all the other dots create?
That no matter how I live my life
and what's inside my heart
I have already been dealt
a hand by fate.

Questions I Secretly Keep

Along the thoughts that step forward
then quickly leave.
I keep questions
I hold in secret asleep.
Breathing within the vines
of all my scattered hopes.
Even when lightning strikes
my field of vision, these questions,
I secretly keep.

When the day comes
I will softly smile in anticipation.
The gaze of my eyes
will meet your own.
I will no longer wait to wake
the questions I keep.
In full daylight out of secret
they will climb.
No longer
in my thoughts alone.

Sometimes I hear these questions
simply fading away.
Beneath the green grass under my feet.
Pushed completely out of my mind's
field of vision.
Until the truth in my heart
awakes to hear
these questions again, repeat.

Exhaled as Poetry

I feel your tenderness underneath my bare feet;
see my face as a reflection
of a flame, in your eyes.
One thousand teardrops
fell from your heart,
love swallowed each one.
Tasting comfort inside a smile,
a heart grows fond of drinking
love's replies.

Your words fall as leaves
into the river of my heart's desire,
come to life
when I exhale them as poetry.
Each breath I take
rises against another,
creating feelings inside my heart,
ringing in tones listening to each thought;
bringing such a lovely peace to me.

I am embraced by breezes
stirred from a lasting love
that has grown strong like an oak tree.
It bends but never breaks.
Love now sails as notes
pouring from my lips.
My heart leaps with joy
and sings replies perhaps unheard,
but felt with each breath
I take.

Underneath a Whisper of Darkness

Underneath a whisper of darkness,
lies a candle burning.
Fear and suspicion caress the flame.
Invisible hands of time
lay at rest and waiting.
Softly murmuring in words of ink
across the page.

The sound of scars echo
in the whisper of darkness.
Breathing in the essence of the flame.
Time rolls words
in the crystal ink of pain
upon the pages of the heart
that still remains.

Experience fades to colors whispering
in the darkness.
Softly playing with edges
of the flame.
Time slowly spreads the ink
across the pages
of an existence eagerly awaiting
to live again.

Underneath a whisper of darkness,
lies a candle waiting.
Within a heart held prisoner
by a mind.
Caressed by scars
of fear and suspicion.
Deeply engraved by the invisible
hands of time.

Heels of Remembrance

Capricious waves push at my hands,
show how much you mean to me.
Do you remember
how we used to play instead of talk?
I would dress for my day
while you stood with your back turned,
considering if you should go ahead
and celebrate the details
of a few minutes drawn in chalk.

Our eyes look down the road
at the reasons we have to be grateful.
Looking at skid marks left in place
from better times.
A wisp of smoke considers
those heels I wore for you
That tore down the walls
in our bedroom many nights.
Do those memories fill your mind?

Just a little air to breathe was all we needed
inside of this our warmth.
So we could feel the joy of love without labels.
You stepped back and so did I
to sip from the glass of our glow.
Because we thought routine
had taken all control
Leaving nothing
on our table.

I find I cannot breathe the air and this drink
has lost its glow.
Have you forgotten how we used to play?
Where is that wisp of smoke
that remembers me in heels
that tore down the walls in our bedroom
as we undressed our day?

On the Cufflinks of Beating Hearts

I always knew that lightning
could split the sky
as the world stared calmly
at all that lies inside distraction.
That just a touch from the strongest hands
takes the breath away
from all that has been written
on the edges
of thoughts of satisfaction.

I have always felt the shadows of the night
even though they were hidden
from the innocence of my caring view.
They are just as bold in the morning
like silvery crystals flying
by sweet lovers
as glints fading into a powerless time
we once pursued.

Constant tears
have been inches apart
from the concern felt for foolish reasons,
when what is unknown is revealed.
Moreover, I have always known
that anguish is felt by beating hearts
when everything carried on their cufflinks
silently cries not to be real.

However, I did not know
that lightning is arranged
in wild waves we feel in our sleep,
as it does not strike disturbingly.
Nor, that the shadows of the night
can come unmasked
to trace its fingers as an exhale
across hearts with destinations
unknown to me.

Hope's Perfume

Like forgotten lines dancing around love
that never bloomed,
knowing not where to start or end.
You will know when you look
at the blurs that form
when crossing the night
once again.

Stretching across the lines are flowers
that once planned to brush the lips
of all the answers
you need.
Yet, the smile on your face
could change the mind,
overwhelm the heart
of destiny.

In the distance I see rain
coming down from the air of dreams
full of laughs and smiles
taking flight.
I stare for such a long time
knowing it could all soon go away,
and my heart cries
as I write.

Forgotten lines cut into winds
that wander
but have always been right there
dancing around love
that could bloom.
Without moving far off
or crossing the night
we can still smell
Hope's perfume.

Whisper To Me

Come whisper to me, remarkable words
when evening cascades to a sigh.
I want to still hear your voice
echoing against my skin
after I kiss you
goodnight.

Encircle my world with the sound of your thunder.
Listen to my pulse throb as it resounds.
You can measure each beat,
matched with your own.
In the way you make
my heart pound.

Come and place your hand on the small of my back.
Leave me with your calm and serene air
so that when I lie down alone
close these eyes……….
I can still feel you there.

Walking In the Shadows of Why and How

For years, I guess the glass I used
to see me on the outside
revealed a clear sky
singing at one timid glance,
from an occasional nod,
I called my own.
In some remembrance
of this cross I wear
for my thousandth second chance.

I wonder if the truth of my mortality
has chosen now to meet
with the knowledge lifted from this
Phoenix's ashes.
Or is it just as plain
as the untouched places
where loneliness gives rise
and fancy strays
to self-inflict
a thousand lashes

I look once again into the glass
see myself on the inside
Full of love and the wonder
of the here and now.
With the occasional nod,
I call my own
I bravely cross the line
I drew in sand
long ago.
Walk within the shadows
of why and how.

If I Could Paint the Sky

I could never say
I would like for you to be stronger
than the wind or rain.
You shine
even when raging tempests
are knocking
on the door of time.

I can hear passion in your voice
when you tell me
you remember
how I sang I love you
in your ear
and called you my Muse
that whispers words of love
over my shoulder.

I look into the window of your soul
see my own
smiling back happily
in the reflection of a mirror
that ripples stronger every day.
I can see myself there, still singing to you
within this art I write in my tears
of joyful rain.

If a painting of the skies could open up
a tidal wave of hidden emotions
that would change life for the better,
I would learn how to paint for you.
Then you could breathe in
how I feel when you touch me
each time you look at my painting again.

I would never expect you to be stronger
than the wind or rain
and I know you don't expect me
to paint the sky. So for now
I will write the words of love
you whisper over my shoulder
and sing I love you,
in your ear, until the day
I die.

Untying the Bonds From Our Wings

Is not comfort expressed
in what we look for everyday?
When our fingers move through fire
to untie the bonds from our wings
so we can become the form
of everything.

When old thoughts are found on pages
containing imaginary stairs
do we find that our eyes lie to us
about worlds we will find there?
Or do we just like those new beginnings
where all is well and fair?

Each day I tell you that I am not the one
who in time will disappear.
Yes, inside I move eagerly towards trust
and forwards I dive full into the sky.
But here with you,
I find to be most dear.

Night and day we climb hills to see the sun
and all its possibilities.
Yet we never blink an eye or stare
at the dreams visible to us all.
Perhaps, we are afraid to open the door
to our own imagination's call.

Taste of You

The bond between us
does not quite speak to the stars
as precious carvings
but as seeds of happiness.
Here you see me in thought
rearranging reflections inside a message
held in glass.

Far away I hold my breath
then let it out to chase dream-filled sleep.
Soft sighs escape
streaming through the night
in shells of kisses
moving ultimately to form this lovely
smile I keep.

Quivering inside my dreams
are elaborate colors
that dance on my tongue.
I taste them as whispers of you.
The bond between us does not quite
speak to the stars, but here
in my dreams is sung.

Imperfect Creatures

The spinning of the Earth is never interrupted
for anyone.
Although, faces of men whisper of experience
between ideas that come undone.

Deep questions slide into all we know to be,
step right in.
Yet, we do not hesitate to look away,
when their hours begin.

Looking back at the summer of our lives,
were we supposed to hold hands?
Perhaps we never tried, or merely gave up
in the end.

Just another minute or two try's not too smile
when reading what's been said.
We wait for justice, and then roll over
playing dead.

Settling in, we do not mention lessons
learned from each moment.
Is this not a step towards
what lies underneath our torment?

Are we running out of time and a foot behind,
because we do not care?
Do we only commit to that which comforts
our own air?

Sometimes I doubt if we closed our eyes for a second
we would see the entire picture,
perhaps because, we refuse to see ourselves
as we are,
Imperfect Creatures.

Night and Day

She quickly took the fiery sun from the astounded sky
Replaced its brightness with the moon
The sky was stunned for the briefest of moments
Until the air was filled with a sacred tune

A sacred tune sang by the dazzling stars of silver
flooding the sky with radiant light
Emanating from their hiding places in heaven
Filling the sky with wondrous delight

Soon, the astounded sky forgot about the fiery sun
In peaceful bliss it smiled and listened
Now fascinated by the glowing moon and sacred tune
Sang by the silver stars that glistened

Without warning she returned and quickly took the moon
Replaced the sacred tune with fiery light
The sky was stunned for the briefest of moments
Then filled with wondrous delight

I Have Waited As a Bird

My sky yields heroes of long ago, felt as strange sensations.
They take control of all I have ever known to be
with eyes that watch what comes this way
from those faces my sun cannot see.

Memories of them lie anchored above a line of tangled trees.
With branches full of doves of hope that softly sing.
Lingering declarations into the light of dawn
in their perfect campaign, voices ring.

I have waited as a bird in a cage who dreams to freely fly
here sleeping while the world moves me to wake.
By dipping a pen into the ink of my veins
creating outlines for me to take.

My restless heart beats swift, echoes sweetly into my sky.
Into the breezes that yield my heroes of long ago
to come take control of all I know to be
help me to discover what is so.

I have been here as a shadow poured into a secret cage
calling on fate and chance to come and rescue me.
My heroes of long ago never held the key
I could fly if the sky I would just see

Dancing Moonlight

Misty moonlight falls on dancing waters
shimmers as it plays.
Lights the fall of a gauntlet's challenge
called the sunrise
of the day.

Straining beams of iridescence, quietly appear
changing in a glow.
Accumulating dust from a starlight's sphere
a brilliant sparkling
from long ago.

A splash of velvet is the midnight sky
cradling our moon.
Softly singing the sweetest lullaby
knowing the challenge
is ending soon.

Streaks of crimson, fiery red appear
across the velveteen.
The moonlight's dancing end is near.
The sun again
is seen.

Sleeping Souls

I shall bound triumphantly into a time to come.
Drink of waters none other has ever tasted.
A serene and silent seer
I shall then become.
Into the aching hearts of men
with visions still unread.

Brilliant stars will bloom, which once were faded.
Sleeping souls retracing steps
of a time before their skies were jaded
by those errors made in judgment.
Stealing lives
into a dark misstep.

I shall then lie outside myself
and watch to see.
Those aching hearts drinking waters I have tasted.
A serene and silent seer I will remain and be
while sleeping souls regain the light
they thought once wasted.

Scarcely Did I Turn Away

I thought I saw you as the shadow of my lover's heart
In the hills where the seasons changed today
Waving gently in the wind,
as if to impart
You were the one I look for, everyday

I thought I saw you in the purest flame, gazing back at me
Observing me there helpless in your stare
Yielding glances back at you,
just hoping I would see
My lover's heart, in the light flickering there

I looked for you in the rising tide and waited for its fall
Thought I saw you on the crest of a wave
Heard you in the echo
of a lonesome seagulls call
Seeking out the mate, his heart craves

Scarcely did I turn away and stop looking everywhere
Every waking hour I found anew
I saw you looking back
from the eyes of a face I loved
and already knew.

No Explanation Needed

The moon hangs above two lovers
never fading
from all they want.
Their lips speak a language
of their own.
There need be no explanation
of the urges articulated
between them,
twisting and turning as the misty morning
makes itself known.

They have been pulled under waves
crashing through their fingers
and lingering on their tongues
as love.
Altering how they hold each others heart
within the soil of their being,
worn as a scent displayed as beauty
that can only be
from heaven above.

A walk of response places in full view
conversations that cannot
be denied.
Their hearts overflow with sweet passion
face to face,
remembering how the moon hung sweetly
singing stories of adoration
above them
never fading
from this precious place.

Silent Tears

Have you ever heard the silence of a tear
On an ocean's restless wave?
Or seen a soul
steadily face his fears
to walk on roads unpaved.

Did you ever feel the haze
of someone's pain
inside your own heart too?
Walked their path of dark and rain
held it all inside of you.

Could you ever dream another's dream
Until that dream came true?
Closed your eyes
until it seemed
that dream belonged to you.

If you can see and feel
and know this fear,
hold inside all this and more,
then you can dream a silent tear
to rest on the ocean floor.

Unfathomable

Did you give yourself to the river's edge,
then wish you were here.
When the morning hour blossomed into a gleam.
Are you now afraid my love
will not pull you through
when your hands are reaching out
for your dreams?

Last night you walked deep within the shadows of distress.
The expression on your face astounded me.
However, I saw contentment in your eyes
until the very end
and although I could see your heart bleeding
you reached for nobody.

You are a beautiful yet unfathomable burning flame to me.
I am a moth captured within your light,
following your footsteps on to that river's edge
hoping you will not give yourself up
without a fight.

On My Telling All

On my telling all, the skies counted my last breath
as if, the beginning flowed within a smile.
Exquisitely existing in the windows of our lives
in rooms where we speak of things
ancient, yet known inside of our hearts,
all the while.

I have known different dimensions within my soul
other lands with lovely blue seas.
Is it not evident when you look into my eyes?
I am reminded of a love unforgettable
incredibly dear scenes I hold in precious jars
of my memories.

Endless thoughts reveal answers already known,
a wisdom carried in the mist untold.
Sailing into all that you think lies before you.
Circling to stand alone with the heart
that once existed in the windows of our lives
in the rooms we withhold.

Let the Clouds Watch Them Fly

Let the clouds up in heaven watch the wings of time
while our hearts pull down the shades.
Listen, as they claim them as their very own.
Forgotten like flowers in the wind
our petals will not fade.

Time will stand still and there will be no change.
Our hearts will stand in youth.
Walking softly within a tender strength
bright lanterns that will silence
Time's wings of truth.

Our eyes will sweetly smile at silver threads of life
knowing they will never ever age.
Rewriting our own history on either side
without those heavy wings of time
brushing on the page.

The wings of time demand; tirelessly they seek
a taste of life upon their tongue.
Let the clouds up in heaven watch them fly
our hearts pulled down the shades
once again, we are young.

Etching the Sadness

Strange sounds quietly etch from under places
no one ever wants to chance.
Calling out softly to those who can hear them
in a repetitive wistful chant.

Speaking of darkness in voices unknown
Faintly crying out to be heard
Telling sad tales to those who can hear them
Without ever saying a word

Lonely winds reverberate around misty cold
Stirring the etching of sound
Seeking the spirits of those who can hear them
Wherever they may be found

A touching of minds in wistful repetitive chants
Stirring the sound of misty cold
Quietly etching into the hearts who hear them
The sadness of their souls

Where My Soul Bleeds

I am looking at black ink waking up the words that cut through me
While praying, they form a message that sends relief
I want to scream out that this is my world I love so deeply
And that every page is the ground
Where my soul bleeds

Tell me is it less fair to extend a soul so drained that it no longer sings
Yet still rises shyly to offer a quiet refrain you will never forget
Do the tears that are folded into a new day
Become ignorant so much so that they
Drown your spirit

If I wrote you a love letter, would you search the world for our destiny
Perhaps finding words full of vibrant colors that spin on the truth
Or would you get discouraged with my right hand
For delaying the proud breezes you wish
To feel here in wonder

I am looking at black ink racing through my veins
Let me take the time to create a story that will comfort every page
Of this world I love so deeply because rare is the heartbeat
That overcomes that which is taught by time to walk
On the definition of a kiss

My thoughts crumble into sweet passion waking black ink
Until my heart is bathed in a constant notice from time and space
Although my words are never spoken
Bits and pieces of them enjoyed the last time the ink whispered
Onto pages where my soul bleeds

Moving Within Your Arms

I searched for release
looking at arms saying move
within the magic of me.
Morning brought flames of reason
down to earth
to walk a long road of trust
filling empty spaces
I could see.

Certainly, as love has a rhythm
and my lips knew the pleasure
it bestowed.
Holding in the sound
was much more than I could bear
and nothing would keep me
waiting
to feel its flow.

I found a companion
who lit a fire under heartbreak
until it drifted
into a twilight unknown.
Awakening the child inside me
to breathe in a new brightness
of peace,
heartbreak was gone.

You are where I found release, never hesitating
to give enough to fill the empty spaces
with trust.
Certainly, as love has a rhythm
my lips are bound
to the flow,
move within your arms,
I must

The Coldest Moves

I watched you make one of the coldest moves in front of our reflection.
You plunged through billowing smoke
into areas that lacked any expression at all.
I saw you shift away into various shades of pictures
then run shrieking using all that you had seen as an excuse.
While all the while, I was arranging to tour the fields of you.

I saw headlines printed in places so that they became
more than just this morning's declarations.
I really liked how you always understood
all the tiny little windows you said they held because this is how
you knew everything that was happening.
Yes, you knew it all.

There were hundreds of experiences I could hear asking me why
you were making the coldest moves.
Yet, you acted as if you never heard them.
Still, I saw the look in your eyes
the minute they approached.

Somehow, I could tell you knew what you saw smiled and looked forward
to not hearing what we both needed to say.

All I could do was shake my head, begin to face more puzzling hours
filled with only you and your insistence that I adjust the temperature of the air
you had frozen.
I wondered how anyone could stand and look at you,
not be startled by who you are.

Blurs of agitation too strange for even me to identify
looked over my shoulder with excitement.
They were not there to inhale my perfume
only to seek out my scars. The scars that visit my heart
from time to time to remind me they can still hold my arms back
from reaching out to you.

Even though you laid right next to me we could no longer find each other
in the billowing smoke issuing from our breath.
Ice had begun to form between our hearts
within the coldest moves. There we lay in the darkness
both of us looking for the best place to hide.

Take my word for it, this was not an illusion.
I swear I saw cold clouds
hanging over the bed laughing at you and me.
Because we didn't have the faintest idea
the darkness wasn't real or how close we lay
to what could make us warm again.

Where Chance Takes its Warmth

Through all the ways I feel while every other explanation
clouds my mind, to be with you now
still fades into highlights as the music of my soul.

Tinted bit by bit by what is lost is tomorrow, bathed in bright tracks
everyone can see leaving
as I tried to for years and years.

Dancing in the air are thoughts that do not know
your name, with voices
breathing doubt into my senses.

Now, will endless seconds share the same sky
with the prelude that resonates
from everything I know?

Does a chance watch a veil climb the stairway of daydreams
with eyes
that give what is inside
of me away?

While I long to call what runs around me, only minutes
of which I have no control,
and like a giant oak
I bend against my grain.

After circling through all the ways I feel
and dancing in the air with these thoughts;
I find everything
has become tinted bit by bit
by what is found today.

So now I watch darkness
escape up the stairway of daydreams
while chance takes its warmth
from the veil as it falls.

Still, while I may long to call what we are,
miles away from love,
I find myself following
all the ways
I feel about you.

A Sound I Could Drink

My heart pretended
you were a sound
I could drink
when I went searching
for golden lines full of surprise.
When I walked towards you,
my ears tasted the beat of the earth
and it began to turn
in reverse.

Ringing clear were hundreds of memories
I had kissed freely,
known as all the things you did.
Then in came the rushing sea
crashing into my mind
with waves of everything
you have ever said.

Therefore, I waited by a tree
that had shown its shadow
as being all that I could ever need.
However,
when I looked inside myself,
I found my heart
cold and bare.

A sight I have now become
but there is one thing I surely know.
I could never push aside
the sound of you I drink
from all these golden lines.
My ears will walk
towards you and taste
this beat
until I make you mine.

A Forgotten Era

There are tantalizing visions of an era long forgotten
by the ones who remember the days
of sweet music drifting onto the verandahs
from the imaginations and hearts of ones who played.

Echoing laughter resounds from ivy covered walls
touched by the distant memories that pass
through the cracks left unnoticed by shimmers of light
falling on the sweet summer grass.

A wild crimson rose still grows upon the dim edges
of the latticework now peeling with age.
A remnant of immense beauty, pristinely perfect
still opening its blooms to the stage.

Incessant tales of the wonderful feelings brought to light
as the lovely music lifts to the sky
brings every heart to sing as if they know the tune
these memories have left you and I.

Night Enters With Curious Feet

With curious feet the night enters with beauty in her eager eyes
As love speaks to the ocean of hearts, she has touched
The moon glides by quietly before the eyes of men
And I can see your face held by the fingers
Of my hope, once again

In the eyes of peaceful angels with shining hair of molten gold
I can see those shores of all great happiness and joy
Held by a loyal hand, proclaiming there is love
And such a sweet delight rains down
To my heart, from above

I stand here within the comfort of my silken thoughts of you
While such unmatchable tenderness appears in place
Speaks to me of memories I can always find
While breathing in night's sheer beauty
With my own heart in kind

I see your face, if only for a moment, as the other half of me
As I lay here watching night enter with curious feet
Love sweetly touches my heart in a rush
Tells me to close my tired eyes
Sleep, dear one, shush

Under the Veil

You lifted the veil between the worlds known by many
to walk a rarely trod path, chosen by few.
Seeking to find an existence somewhere in between
instead, you found a world with different rules.

You were drawn in to a mysterious place of allure
where the wolves howl at the moon,
paying homage to the glorious face of delight
while listening to the stars sweet tune.

Each new corner you rounded brought sights anew
sometimes frightening in their glare.
Glowing eyes emerged from the brush in the forest
revealing creatures from ancient nightmares.

The glow of the moonlight brought visions so fair
of maidens and knights on wild steeds.
You watched in awe and wonder as they fell in love
and honor brought them to their knees.

You walked further and further away from the world
of which we all know and understand.
Finding freedom to embrace the mysteries of life
your imagination at your command.

Now the time has come to return to this world
you know and understand well.
Come enlighten us all with the tales you can weave
tell us all, what is under the veil.

Quiet of the Offing

Look yonder at the graceful misty suggestions
delivering a gentle welcoming gain.
Evanescent, yet so remarkably memorable,
infused with the kiss of rain.

A fine gossamer glaze of crystalline blue
creates a jubilant rhapsody
vigorously dancing within the rushing embrace
of the passion, known as the sea.

Flawless perfection, delicately fragile as porcelain
unfaltering, lines of exquisite detail.
Quietly content the eye of the beholder
on a stately sensational scale.

There is splendid comfort in the quiet of the offing
as the cherished waves rush ashore.
Appealing to all of our tender hearts and minds
compelling the joyful need for more.

Storms

A lonesome figure stood upon the crashing waves
extended arms to the darkest skies.
Screaming out her fury at the heavens above
for the bitter storms, she had survived.

Tears streamed from weary eyes so tired of battle
small shoulders shook in agony
cursing the very things that made her stronger
as this, she could not see.

Why me? She moaned and wailed in a mournful tone
hot fear still gripping her heart
while forgetting that she was alive and well to cry
the most incredibly, important part.

Those bitter storms will come and they will pass
they will never stay too long.
Remember when you are screaming out in fury
it is The Storms that make you strong.

Ours

I chase the blazing sun on the wings of a gentle breeze
with my soul, freely open and unconfined.
Listening to the rhythm of the harmony of trees
singing songs of release
to all mankind.

I am never fazed by rain that pours in torrents
when my skies are black as coal.
No fear does flashes of lightening warrant
with this song I hear
kept in my soul.

I carry wisdom within my heart, found as I chase
the blazing sun, on these gentle wings.
Holding inside the rhythm of a trees embrace
in this melody
to you, I softly sing.

No secrets do I hold inside of me, yet I cannot be held.
I am yours and still I am my own.
Chasing the blazing sun as I am so compelled
returning always
to sing to you my song.

In Kind

Tracing shadows with the powerful hand of Fortuity
Watering paper roses with tears
Inscribing verses with the sharpest knife
That cut through the heart of me
Grieving, yet not daring
To show my fear

Sorrow's quietly weeping and knows not why
Listening to murmuring voices
Speaking from faces that smile and cry
Like flames in the wind
Burning ceaselessly
Without choices

Lending my being to all impressions I feel
Surrounding this spirit of mine
Standing open with a bleeding heart, which kneels
To the murmuring voices
Without choices
In kind

Serenading Your Basis

You are a perfect branch
descending
from yourself.
I have been waiting
at your roots,
trying to find myself.

Which part of your trunk
do I stem from,
I cry out to the moon.
Am I not a part of you
whose flowers
are in tune?

I am sharing needful moments
full of sensations anew;
becoming naked
with each breath I take,
singing a song
of truth.

Staring into forever
my heart pounds
with hopes and dreams.
I am waiting at your roots,
with beauty bursting
at my seams.

You are a perfect branch,
no need to conform.
I am here
serenading your roots
to become your flowers
that adorn.

Poetic Showers

If ever there were no secret depths
inside the corners
of a heart,
perhaps lips would not
whisper words
with no preconceptions.
We could paint the air we breathe,
gentle colors that softly speak
to the mind
in a misty lullaby's reflection.

If we could swim within our words
touching gray areas
with kisses of time
perhaps, we could gather waves
to last throughout the years.
In the dark of night,
our hearts would blush,
as they existed side by side
on the edges
of our atmosphere.

Wherever our hands desired to wander,
unnoticed they would never be,
flaming winds stirring
precious hours.
Once again, we could sleep on beds
of soft words raining down
into all of our emotions
and dream
in poetic showers.

Pages of Me

I left you when the world seemed to play a melody of its own
To seek the brilliant lights of whom I wanted to be
Far below what I knew to be real, before all of my wishes
Turned yellow on all of these pages known as me

I drank in the faces underneath masks hiding their true natures
Saw cunning presume my waves rushed in naive
Expecting that I would never feel my heart breaking in two
When all of their darkness flew in, never to leave

Afraid I was not, as I firmly pressed on, soaring above the scent
Of ancient tears that fell on the horizon of night
Drowning themselves in all the final beauty that remained
Before faces changed and turned from the light

I saw broken mirrors holding a silence that quickly turned away
Before all its breath followed brokenness in kind
They were touched by fingertips seeking merely to listen
To endless space, silence creates in your mind

In the distance, sounds try escaping the smiles of gypsy songs
As one and the same, they invaded their peace
With glorious riches that have stormed into stars of past
Remembered dreams that brought sorrow relief

I came back to you when I possessed the truth on my breath
Knowing I had parted from whom I wanted to be
Without you, all of those brilliant lights were not brighter
They had turned yellow on all these pages of me

One By One We Feel the Breezes

One by one we feel the breezes
that soothe us musically
like a breath of silver wings.
Rivers fade into themselves
leaving expressions we understand
yet do not quite notice.
We chase shadows into hidden corners
when night falls;
lie them close
just to hear them ring.

We desire to touch another's name
but when we close our eyes
we are carried away.
The answers we find are reflected
on our fingertips as scars
returning to show more of us
that our time has come.
So we bend like weeping willows
again inspired
by come what may.

Wisdom spirals breathtakingly,
rains down
divided by our faith.
The hand of fortune confounds us,
deafens our ears
to what we believe.
Dawn breaks and we yearn
for what is impossible
to live over again.
Yet, one by one we feel the breezes
that soothe us
musically.

Beneath A Naked Flame

Beneath a naked flame, there lies all the hidden resolution
I heard him softly sing to you my friend.
You bowed your head in a silken thread of absolution
while spilling forgetful darkness
from your hands.

Are your eyes dim because your dreams are distant?
To you I could hear him softly sing.
You bowed your head to escape from existence
then closed your burning eyes
on everything.

Above your line of sight a patient angel is there waiting
he sang to you, although you did not hear
If you will unbow your head, stand still anticipating
Open up your burning eyes
all will be clear.

Beneath a naked flame, there lies your own contentment.
I know because I felt the burn in his song.
If your silken thread holds onto your resentment
your eyes will burn in darkness
your life long.

Language of Desire

Finding myself within a language
that lives inside
the grain of spheres
containing spirits of desire.
My pulse raced with a freedom
not caring to resist
the deliciousness of fire.

I traveled through rooms
where love songs
echoed from the roar of lions.
Sometimes I wandered as a lady fair
who steadied herself
only to disappear
on the horizon.

Descending from speech,
each breath I took
was cast upon the swift currents
where hearts
are often drowned.
I came face to face with fire
collided safe and sound.

Can you hear the words I speak
in this language
known as the spirit of desire?
Does your pulse race
as my own,
not caring
to resist the fire?

Shadows Seek My Eden

I know of something acquainted
with the nearest shadows
seeking to stand in my Eden.
Seen as flames
my footsteps have gone from this world
I no longer taste their freedom.

The cold hard ground checks my validation,
keeps me here every day.
Beautiful places like that of my Eden
make passion felt even more,
losing the mask of my face,
slip sliding away.

All the beautiful seals are removed from my bells.
However, I still hear them ring.
My feet once danced as unbound flames
in my lovely Eden.
Until shadows sprang from pages
and began to sing.

Moments are erased revealing thoughts,
opening the heart
when the earth hangs on a day's silence.
Questions rise then crumble
into the nearest shadow's hands that fight
my splendid Eden's wildness.

Wrapped Around Instinct

A shifting veil of shadows
filled my vision
as if requiring breath aimlessly.
I drew fire into my veins
as my suitor,
when I sought out release.

Looking down upon the back
of my fingers
Warm contentment followed hopefully.
Picking up my hand,
understanding flamed
this fire in me.

A caress pledged half a dream.
Bit my lip suggestively.
Sweet and gentle touches
became phantoms
of hope,
welcoming in, seductive pleas.

Instinct wrapped around a veil
of shadows.
Found everything ever wanted.
Desire left kisses
on my brow,
whispered cries that taunted.

My soul gazed pleasures
state of mind,
took a deep breath of me.
Drawing fire into my veins
as my suitor,
I gave myself….shamelessly.

Under the Skies of You

You are all I need,
when you look at me, I am invincible.
Hold me closer,
no need to chase,
more than once you have loved me
under the skies of yourself.

A mere whim would never
change my mind
but you wake me up
when your face
searches for release
in my eyes.

You are to the whole of my being
every moment I place
as precious
with the ink of my pen.

I cannot let a single day go by
without touching the sands
we call ours
when they appear on the shores
of every part of me.

You are all I need,
when you look at me, I am invincible.
Hold me closer, your arms whisper
the rhythm of me.

No need to chase, come and hold me
under the skies of yourself.
I want to linger here
Enclosed in the love we make.

While You Held My Heart

Last night you rocked me to sleep
while you held my heart.
You took your place
and looked upon my faded seas,
renewed my thirst for life.
Within all the sounds sublime
and oh so sweet
your voice fills the eyes of my night.
I am turned to take and take
each move of love
you lay
at my feet
never forgetting a single line
in my hunger.

To hear you call me a creature
over-flowing with
soft sounds
makes me want to let them continue
gliding from my mouth
forevermore.
They tumble like ocean waves
of thought
from my heart and soul
to become the stars of heaven's floor.

Filling the Emptiness

In my ways this pen
has always found a reason
to find itself in between my hands.

Sometimes I take the time
to ask if this is it, when truth rushes in
to fill my spirit as ink swirls
upon my skin.

I am not afraid of storms that breathe
into this poetry I write,
because all its winds lead me
to those places, where I can feel.

Does a constant need bring excitement
leaving us sailing away on songs
lying at the bottom of our hearts?
Is this the place we roam?

A place where memories keep hoping
we will let them in as they surround the years
rising to sing in a key
our voices never meant to sing again.

Do not tell me I break the rules
when I try and turn the wheel of fate.
You know I will always be the one,
trying to fill the empty air
with song.

Tell me, how does one close up emptiness
when it's been there so long
even the world thinks it's part of the air
they breathe?

In my ways this pen wakes me,
gives me back my heart.
Delighted, I find myself wondering
if I should sign my name,
or pour this emptiness I filled,
back into my pen
and part.

I Set Out to Write All That I Am

Walking down a hall of splendor,
simplicity smiles from the edges fragilely.
My eyes are enchanted by empty hearts,
gliding to transform their fates, aflame in all their need.

Closing in are hands from years
falling through the comforts, I know nothing of.
Quickly clouding my field of vision,
I see what I cannot dream of ever promising in any sound of love.

Fires burn and invitingly wake me
to stand visible to all aching hearts.
Yet I cannot see what they seek to win.
Until, I find I am burning in these halls of splendor
crying with no beginning and no end.

I set out to write all that I am
and found in time I had penned a tale
that left footprints on the souls
of those who had looked into the flickering fire
of my heart, thinking they knew me well.

I Feel You as Soft Touches

I want to see the thoughts
you breathe, hear your words and collect them,
cradled in your honesty.
I could watch the beauty in your eyes
for eternity without ever wishing
to walk away.

You give me your hand
and I close my eyes,
hear the whisper of the sea
and I remember how my heart
has searched for one
such as you knowing I have found my home.

My love,
the world could dance
on the shells of their falsehood
with words
written in beautiful calligraphy
and your words
would continue to run in my veins
like Morse code
tapping out who I am
to me.

You fill my hope chest with your spirit
lifting my head
from the table of where my mind wanders
when I forget
to stop and smell the roses along the way.
Your words
bring precious harmony
into play.

I look through the window of my heart
where you
have pressed your lips
on a photograph of your words
and I feel you as soft touches
on my soul.
I collect them one by one
to remember,
until you again I hold.

Heard On My Skin

When warm I love you's join affection
our souls
cannot seem to say
it is time to go.
I can see
no journey's end
that will ever prove to me
that forever
could ever think
of leaving this love we stand by.

I hold on tight to your soul
even after
we say goodnight.
Inside my mind, I see visions
looking back at caresses
from your hands
and no door is closed
In my heart
containing any words written
you have not read.

Sometimes life feels like a river
flowing into the dawn
reaching beyond
any love song of passion
clinging to the clouds
I am in.
However, thoughts of you
sail me higher
and higher
into beautiful colors
again.

I am left breathless when I see your hands
moving within the realms
of a thousand
I love you's yet to be said.
I can see no journey's end
to this forever
I feel,
as one by one
they are heard on my skin.

More Than I Can Say

I went looking for something different,
maybe embedded in the rooms
of other worlds.
Possibly feelings
contained in oceans,
Drunk
from singing
romantic melodies.

I found skies running backward
and started asking myself
too many questions
about just how
I should be.
Then across my face
ran my inner child
and solved the mystery.

Under my feet, I stepped on syllables
I had charmed
into becoming a song
of the morning.
Just to watch them staring back
into the sea of my soul
on pages requiring nothing
from me.

I went looking for something different,
entranced
in complete curiosity.
What I found was a flower
unwinding each petal
into the light of day.

Embedded in the rooms of other worlds
there are winds
that imprint pleasure in shades
that cry out to the ego
in sudden breaths
and feelings
contained in oceans
burning brighter
than anything I have
ever said.

Circle of Satisfaction

There is no time, in my eyes,
spent with you
that contain shadows,
warranting hopelessness or a magic potion.
Our sweet water is never lost
in what lays within
the music
streaming from our hands.

As if in a circle of satisfaction,
we talk in retrospect,
seeking comforting remnants
of what we brought to each others arms.
Measured spaces sit upright
on the shores of who we are,
yet still,
we are the same.

The whispering cries of love and hope
slowly pace
outside our doors.
We smile at memories
ascending to meet them
in the truest beauty.
What more
could we ask for?

Music to our ears so sweet,
is time slipping
where it's supposed to.
Why would we run and ask for more
knowing one day again
we will be
face to face?

Spirit of a Thousand Winds

I thought I had told you, I have never
loved someone like this,
or felt the touch of a spirit
like a thousand winds
wrap around my moments in this way.

Look me in the eye and taste the passion
of this wine that pours from my heart.
You will then know the chemistry
that makes up the rhythm of truth
in these words I speak to you.

Listen to how much easier the rain falls
because we hear calmer waters
when we sail on the river
of our sweetest emotions.

I thought you knew how I dream
of drawing the curtains of love's intoxication
across our windows
and calling off our search for different skies.
I was sure you understood
how my fingertips trace one hundred places
on your face that I love more each time
I seek them out with my eyes.

I thought I had told you,
I have never loved someone like this,
but perhaps I merely spoke these words in my mind.
So I tell you now, I speak them aloud,
to let there be no questions
running in the meadow of everything we feel.
I have never loved anyone
as I love you.

Take my hand
and let's draw the curtains
of love's intoxication across our windows.
Let us shut out the world
and sail on the river of our sweetest emotions.
I will trace those places on your face
that I adore with all I am.
Come wrap me in your spirit
of a thousand winds.

When I Am Away From You

A normal day, I think not, when I am away from you.
This is when my heart races
and I talk too much with my eyes.
Who sees the places that wake up the world
when I walk beside you?
Even ancient stars stare subtlety in silence
at the easy way my thoughts exude
sweet memories of you.

Where are the little rooms where flowers blossom
when I look into the looking glass
that whispers love travels
between you and me?
Why is it when I look into the back of my mind
I find I am drinking in the essence of you
until I am filled with a happiness
full of color that takes
my breath away.

A normal day, I think not, when I am away from you.
Shade may cover the sun
but the memory of your eyes
sings the light back to me.
My beloved, the mere mention of your name
on my lips
takes away any restless shadows
that try and pass into my heart
you see.

You are inside of me as love splashed on the canvas of my day.
It makes no difference if my hand touches your own.
A normal day, I think not,
when I am away from you,
but I know,
I am never alone.

Beyond What is Mentioned

You are there beyond what is mentioned
when I rise from my chair.
Predicting the future
seems to always end in futility.
I could walk with you
through all these words
that are foreign.
But would I find myself burning
in unutterable possibilities?

Anticipation you cannot see in my stride
when I move vaguely along.
Plainly oblivious to all the grass
growing under my feet.
You see me breathing slowly
wonder how soon I will fly
into phrases more pleasing
than tasting honey is sweet.

A temporary distance runs in a curve
beyond what is mentioned.
Your eyes seize the fire
from half-truths you can hear.
Present moment is held in nameless rooms
hid in the dark.
Where you try to read notes
I penned for you there

I move vaguely along planting footsteps
leading to my heart.
Creating a path to free your own
from this distance.
I am not oblivious to the grass
growing under my feet.
When I rise from my chair,
I am anticipating a change
in our existence.

Within the Reach of My Two Arms

Within the reach of my two arms,
my world is exhilarating.
The earth knows I understand,
why it turns.
Gone, are all mere fantasies,
perhaps just as well.
One kiss and I saw smoke,
felt the fire burn.

My thoughts went out searching
for God's desire for me.
On the edges of eventually
and pretty soon.
Found a star that sang this song
into all my views.
Until all that remained inside of me
was you.

Let me show a thousand waves
from a life of happiness.
A kingdom looking back
in wondrous bliss.
I wish to sit awhile, not speak,
just watch the tide.
Stray from a few words,
awakening a kiss.

A piece of life's hair is let down
listening to this song.
Never reaching shadows dancing along.
Yet, it enters the rooms
within my sight,
Bringing you, into the reach
of my two arms.
Regardless of whether
right or wrong.

Tall Green Grasses

We found that tall green grasses kissed our words
when you and I walk together.
Distance could not strip away warmth
from weary ghosts.

Love's beautiful thoughts sweetly entered in to wash
over too many night's realizations.
Easy winds charmed our evening's cries
existence sighed.

We found refuge writing I love you one hundred ways
with yearning hands, silken moves.
Muses smile above the tall green grasses
thus defying logic.

Love's beautiful thoughts, touching tall green grasses
Appreciating our words with kisses
Where we found refuge writing I love you
all existence sighs.

Love on the Breath of Impossibility

Could I be defeated by love so sweet
moving in echoes
across an immense hidden wheel of fate,
spinning memories?
Would the eyes of birds then bid farewell
to contentment
by removing the shroud of flight
finely covering me?

If I sang, a song scarcely heard
on the breath of impossibility,
could someone chime in with a glance of time
returning me to dust?
Or would it never shed into the places
where they set out in ships full of water
from the Fountain of Lust?

I once said the touch of a journey at first value
is held within the heart as a home
where faith has a character of its own.
However, I was not prepared
for the power or vitality of a dream
surviving over the longest time
ever known.

Rising away there in the fields,
I wonder why love leaves
on the air of pain
with its thumbs held out
to the Light of Never.
Can a poet such as I
lengthen what is kept
inside the day when Love's Court
is held lingering within forever?

A blizzard of vacancy is coming down,
filling my heart,
a heart once made of stone.
Yes, I can be defeated
by love so sweet.
It has a character of its own.
I bid farewell to this shroud of flight
and to this impossible
breath of song.

A Delightful Form

I could say my right hand does not believe it is confined
while everything slips through my fingers.
Agree that the usual is not mine to ever know
just so, you will feel comfortable.
There within the skin
which you linger.

I could tell you that I am not hungry for small things
I see most everyone else holding near.
Because I have a spirit that travels quite light
always seeking peace in all that is still.
So you will continue to smile
at me, my dear

Would you still look into my eyes with the same trust
if within mine, you saw a brewing storm?
Working its way into my soul that I could not stop
or would you decide I am a stranger
with a heart you no longer consider
a delightful form.

On the Air of Eternity

You hold the fruit of my pathways
during storms that could chill the shores
of the blackest hearts.
Forming bracelets that encircle my soul
until I am down on my knees
knowing wherever you go I will follow
because I am your other part.

You hold in store a truth that sweeps across me
with a brilliance speaking slowly and softly
like the stars affection for the moon.
My heart beats in solid measure with your own,
same as starlight removes
a shadows downcast of gloom.

You spill into my sleep and kiss me with understanding
behind the blossoming beauty calling from years
of not being held,
breathing life into that which never beat with love.
Until what mattered most
found it adored the kiss finally felt.

My days ripple with the finest occupation of creation,
pressing against my tongue
as a breeze of the sweetest wine.
I hold your words on the air of eternity
and pray they always tell me
you will hold me
whenever I am looking for
all I need to find.

Love's Willingness

What began as a trickle moved forward
into what can never be forgotten
Flying into hearts and souls as faces,
with mysteries that unfold
Holding one another in winds
conveying what they feel
Falling to fit inside a claim,
heaven must uphold

Hands move through walls of water,
beckoning want inside two bodies
Moments hold complexities
until all thoughts they feel as one
Sighs strip the cloth away,
revealing their tomorrows
Paradise comes in waves,
loneliness is undone

Storms of contemplation feel life racing
to repeat the steps they know
As their fingers dance on unmade plans
with places still to go
Gentle touches brush the grounds
of want and need
Forward into now,
love's willingness exposed

Shadows of these days will always
linger in their souls leaving colors
Surrounding the breezes
capturing love's attention waiting
What once began as a trickle
cannot be left behind
Arms outstretched,
love's river anticipating

When Lightning Plays On the Keys of Your Sorrow

Forgive me when lightning plays on the keys of your sorrow
and there is no time for everything you say
to be laid here at my feet.
Still, know that I am here when your inner light
of wisdom catches dust on the frame of your heartbeat
and I will listen through your tears.

On those days when life feels like a flying bird,
do not feel sorry for reaching out
to enlightenment as your lover, please know,
that I understand your need.

There are miles of bedlam that I would love to turn into flowers
on those nights when your sea tumbles restlessly
and those dragons of madness make you burn
the sticks of your destiny.
Instead, I will hold you in my heart
so that you can hear it beat for you,
a breath apart and still the same.
We will drown our souls together
in our own tranquility.

When you hear the call of honor weeping to the heavens above
while leaves of scorn fall upon your head,
I will stand beside you
help you roll away
what stands in front of you.

Let me be the force that drives you from the shadows
of all heartache,
when lightning plays on the keys
of your sorrow. Even though sometimes
there is no time for everything you say
to be laid here at my feet,
always know that my feet still remain here,
next to you.

A Blind Eye

Should you stay and follow the ones that hold you
In a rambling verse of delicate lies
Not visit the grieving spirits with tears overdue
Just to see an approving glance
In a stranger's eyes

Will you hold on the tip of your tongue the words
That rise from the dew of care
To follow an illusion so incredibly absurd
That tomorrow you will not recall
Why you were there

Can you measure your waters by the glow within
Or know what your future holds
If you dance with the one whose aim is to win
Regardless of pain and despair
Within his control

Landscape

To one who's name is written in the faint perfume upon my neck
Your hands gently tend my landscape with their caress
Each and every flower, you gracefully bedeck
In the richest warmth of your undress

You move your morning breezes into the darkness of my night
Until I no longer know the season or present year
Time is of no essence within my sight
Of warmth or cold, I have no fear

To one who's name is written on every single line of my heart
In your ink flowing from the radiance of our eternal sun
Your hands tend my landscape in a world apart
Marked on a calendar of none

The cares of life, waft into silent pieces as they come to light
When your morning breeze moves upon my flowers
Each one you tend with your hand's sight
Forgets these cares of ours

To one who's name is written in my eyes as my master gardener
My flowers will always seek the ink flowing from our sun
My landscape will be your garden harbor
From your breezes, I will never run

Life of a Promise

Silently waiting near the halls of years that have passed
Is the beginning of lost and confused
Calling farewell to yesterday's river of tears
That ran deeper than a mystery
Left unproved

A promise does its best to save the life of a memory
What more noble an expression exists
When there is barely a beginning before the end
Of another day that is born to smile
And dismiss

The tick of a clock changes so much in these halls
Brings the beginning of enlightenment
Bidding farewell to the end of lost and confused
As the memory of the life of a promise
Is infused

About the Author

Neva Flores was born and raised in the warm State of Georgia. She is a mother and a grandmother. She began writing poetry in 2009 and song lyrics in 2010.

Neva has published two other hardcopy books and several e-books.

Prolific writer is probably the best description of this poet/songwriter. Neva has written well over 1200 pieces since she began writing in 2009.

www.ingramcontent.com/pod-product-compliance
Ingram Content Group UK Ltd.
Pitfield, Milton Keynes, MK11 3LW, UK
UKHW041930190726
13854UKWH00004B/1533

9 781105 469466